Soaring Wings

a song of remembrance

by Beverly J. Mick

ISBN: 978-0-9825974-9-1

Published and printed in the United States of
America by The Write Place. Cover and interior
design by Kathie Evenhouse, The Write Place.
For more information, please contact:

The Write Place
709 Main St., Suite 2
Pella, Iowa 50219
www.thewriteplace.biz

Interior art by Kathie Evenhouse.

Copies of this book may be ordered from The
Write Place online at
www.thewriteplace.biz/bookplace

Dedication

This book is dedicated to:

Sylvia L. Mick,
my father's mother,
who treasured local history
and gave me her 1881 edition of
The History of Marion County, Iowa.

and

Richard A. Samuel,
my mother's father,
who enjoyed inventing
personalized light-hearted rhymes
to entertain his many grandchildren.

Preface

The French once claimed Canada and the Mississippi Valley as part of their worldwide empire. They wrote "New France" on the maps of this vast colony and tried to rule it from Montreal in eastern Canada. In the 1730s, when the Fox tribe of Wisconsin resisted their rule, a sharp and bitter struggle began.

To convert this rough conflict into smooth reading, there are several special features in the text. There's a handy list of the three Indian tribes, all of which are known by two names in the story: Fox/Mesquakie, Sac/Saki, and Mohawk/Iroquois. There's also a list of the six Sac and Fox leaders singled out for honor. The story itself employs catchy rhymes to speed the action along and make it easy to memorize— for I would like readers to remember these Indian names. There are Notes at the end filled with enriching details and Classroom Comments for teachers.

For a compact survey of the early French fur trade, with informative maps, see *The Upper Country* by Claiborne Skinner. For the family, consider Howard Sivertson's colorful work, *The Illustrated Voyageur*.

Roster of Names

Three of the tribes in this story are called by two names:

Fox = Mesquakie

Sac = Saki

Mohawk = Iroquois

Six counties in Iowa are named for the following Sac and Fox Leaders:

Fox/Mesquakie Tribe

Wapello

Tama

Poweshiek

Sac/Saki Tribe

Appanoose

Keokuk

Black Hawk

Soaring Wings

a song of remembrance

by Beverly J. Mick

I

In Wapello's grandfather's
grandfather's day,
When the Fox lived in Wisconsin
below Green Bay,

They called themselves Red Earth People, 5
Mesquakie.
Their neighbors, the Yellow Earth People,
were Saki.

When their neighbors' grandchildren's
grandchildren came, 10
Appanoose and Keokuk
would be their names.

In southern Wisconsin
where Portage now stands,
You can visit the heart   15
of the Sac and Fox lands.

It's not the richest country
nature ever made,
But was prized as a short-cut
in the French fur trade.   20

Now the Fox were independent
and didn't always obey
The rules set back in Montreal,
a thousand miles away.

They didn't like traders   25
selling muskets to the Sioux,
And wouldn't let canoes
carrying firearms through.

Though they were a brave, a decisive,
and a resourceful band,   30
They acted like they thought themselves
the owners of the land.

So while they hunted and fished
and harvested corn,
A Montreal plot for their destruction   35
was born.

II

French troops, their Mohawk friends,
and the Fox's Huron foes
Hatched a scheme to shoot the Fox
like helpless fawns and does.   40

They thought they were Big Medicine
and fit to declare
Who could do what
and who could live where.

But hundreds of troops and warriors   45
in Montreal canoes
Are tough to move in secret
to distant rendezvous.

Before they paddled to Green Bay
to spring their sneak attack,   50
Friends had sent warnings
to the threatened Fox and Sac.

So when the Great War Party
reached the Fox's lair,
The corn fields were empty,   55
the wigwams were bare.

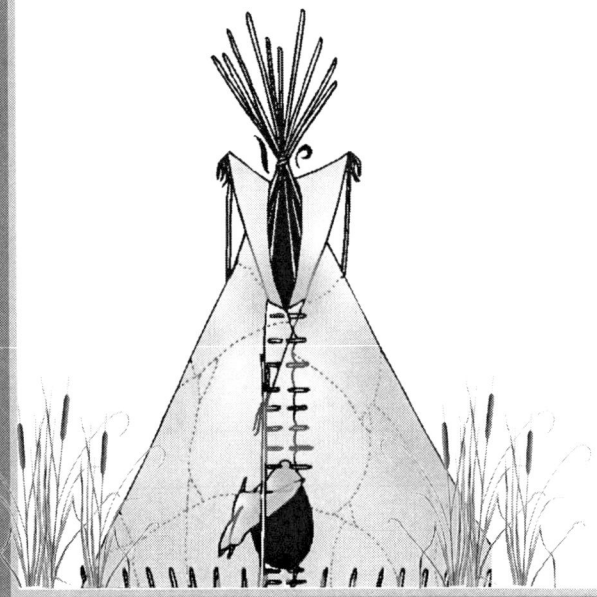

Gone... Gone...
The villagers were gone,
Lying low in Iowa
on the Wapsipinicon.   60

'Neath the springtime snows
of seventeen thirty-five,
The hunted Fox had gone to ground
just to stay alive.

And in an act of kinship   65
you cannot overstate,
The loyal Sac had fled with them
to share their fate.

III

For fresh packhorses,
the French searched far and wide,   70
Hired Chippewa hunters,
and watched for a western guide.

Still, some of their allies
would not venture on
To the Mississippi   75
and unknown lands beyond.

They discovered an old guide
in northern Illinois
Who'd hunted eastern Iowa
with his father as a boy.   80

And following him a hundred miles
to the south and west,
They found where the villagers
had stopped to rest.

Man, woman, and child,   85
the young, the old
Had left their footprints
in the mud and cold.

On the banks of the wandering
Wapsipinicon,   90
You could see where they'd slipped
and stumbled on,

Leaving a trampled track
so deep and so wide
The French and their allies   95
didn't need a guide.

IV

Such weakness put the captain
in a good mood.
He could rest his troops
and look for food. 100

He had eighty troops
and many braves more,
And needed to refill
their empty food store.

He ordered the hired hunters 105
from the Chippewa nations
To bring in meat
to replenish their rations.

"I can tell you," the old guide said,
"what not to do.   110
Don't chase any game
through the land of the Sioux."

The Mohawks muttered,
"It's the Sioux who should fear.
And they will if they try to touch   115
a Mohawk's deer."

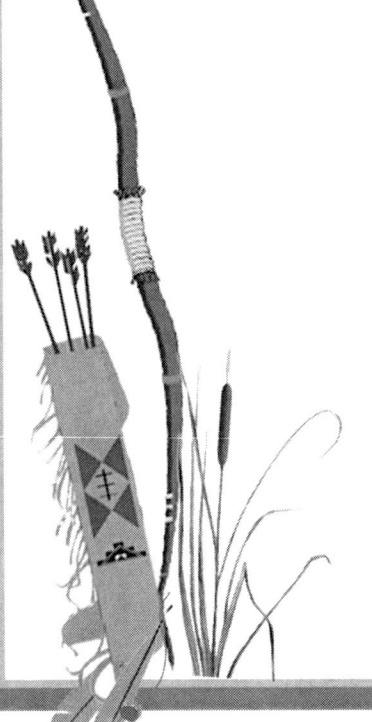

They searched days,
south and north, west and east,
But could find little venison
on which to feast.   120

Perhaps the villagers had eaten
all the deer around.
Perhaps the plan to follow the Fox
had not been sound.

Warriors are not the type   125
to stand and brood.
They'd just hurry and catch the Fox
and eat their food.

V

Fording the Red Cedar
and the swift Ioway,   130
They drew closer to the villagers
day by day.

Like an arrow to its target,
they flew across the state,
Grasping for the Sac and Fox   135
like the hand of fate.

'Cause the villagers' necks
had been trapped in a cord,
They were fleeing toward a stream
they could never ford.   140

It was a mighty river,
wide as a lake,
Blocking the path
they had chosen to take.

Only an eagle   145
with soaring wings
Could cross the Des Moines
in the spring.

VI

Still, bad blood was running
and tempers were hot. 150
The Fox were eating
and the French were not.

Once boastful hunters
sicced their best dogs
After skittery varmints 155
around prairie bogs.

While, kneeling in the icy mire,
the vengeful Huron
Studied roots and bulbs
to find bits to chew on. 160

At the Skunk River,
the old guide began to fail,
Shrinking in his great robe,
looking stooped and frail.

When struggling uphill,   165
he'd shy with a start
As a covey of quail
raced through his heart.

He mourned for his summer bride's
laughs and sighs   170
And the warm glow of fireflies
in her eyes.

It's a mixed blessing,
being a scout with second sight.
By day he saw strange things   175
that disturbed his sleep at night.

In a twisted twig,
a bent tuft of grass,
He saw
a huddled family pass.   180

If a frayed thread
from a lower limb should fall
He saw an old woman shiver
and clasp her shawl.

Night after night,   185
he laced the racks
That cradled children
on their mothers' backs.

He remembered how
he'd helped his mother   190
By lacing up the cradle
of his infant brother.

And that was the theme
of his final dream.
His father came to take him   195
and they left downstream.

VII

The captain kept counting
his troops every morning,
And his allies kept deserting
at night without warning.   200

The chase was so close
that a southern breeze
Brought the scent of fresh campfires
through the trees,

When from a distant ridge   205
in the morning light,
The great bed of the Des Moines
swept into sight.

Shading their eyes,
they caught a gleam   210
Of the far-off, stately,
winding stream.

They'd reached the river
you cannot ford.
They'd earned the king's   215
royal reward!

They loosed their tomahawks
and raised their lances,
And leaped in ancient
victory dances.   220

The smell of venison
was in the air!
They'd surprised the Fox
asleep in his lair!

Exploding from the forests   225
with mayhem and slaughter,
They'd smash those tribes
and toss them in the water.

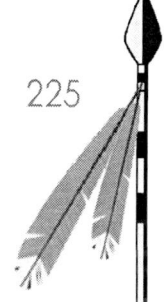

The king's orders were prophetic
and bitter. 230
"Club the Fox. Club the vixen.
Drown the litter."

Fearing their celebrations
might soon be seen,
They disappeared 235
down the nearest ravine.

Hiding in the low creek bed
all the way,
They'd completely surprise
their sitting prey. 240

VIII

There was only one flaw
in their vicious scheme;
The villagers hadn't stayed
to be tossed in the stream.

When they burst from the forest,   245
they caused no fright,
But encountered instead
a puzzling sight.

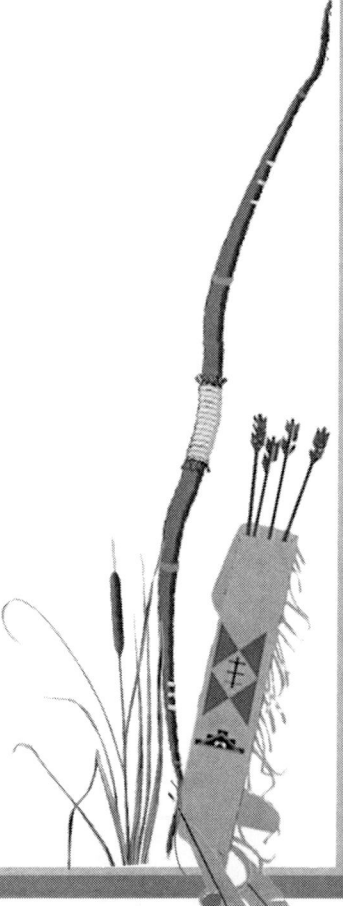

Fifty wigwams
lined the opposite shore   250
Wreathed in the smoke
they had smelled before.

They blinked and stared
and muttered a curse,
But things just went from bad   255
to worse.

There was a fort—a fort!—
on the far-off banks,
A large stockade
of thick wood planks.   260

The troops dropped, dejected,
like wounded birds,
And the captain and the Iroquois
exchanged strong words.

Without wings, all hope of reward   265
was now gone.
They were caught in the cord
they'd been counting on.

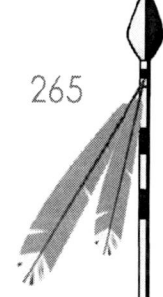

The river was so broad,
so wide, so vast;   270
How could the little villagers
have passed?

The hungry Hurons
rocked and grieved.
It wasn't fair;   275
they'd been deceived.

And to add to their sense of doom
and gloom,
They discovered the logjam
that afternoon.   280

Some Mohawks got over
and started a fight,
But the Fox's fort
was thick and tight.

The captain growled,   285
"Save your breath.
They can stall over there
'til we starve to death."

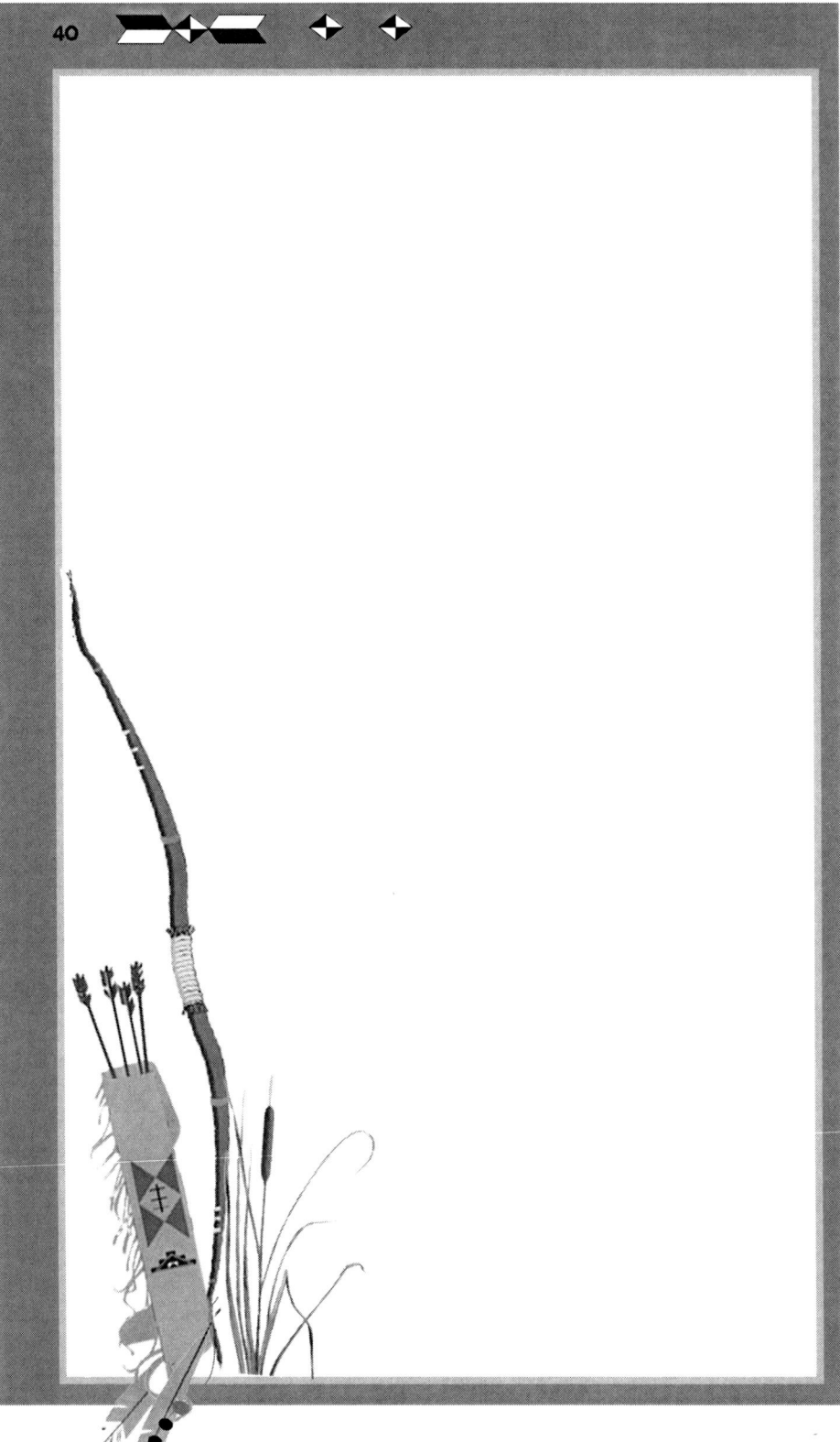

IX

When the morning mist melted
from the river at dawn,   290
The French, the Iroquois,
and the Huron were gone.

Turning to face
more March winds and rain,
They left the Des Moines'   295
sleepy domain.

Limping back to Wisconsin
where it had all begun,
Eating their dogs, their horses,
and their moccasins.   300

Around a thousand campfires
the question vexed:
If the captain had devoured the Fox,
who would he eat next?

A little servant of a middle servant   305
of far-off kings
Still has responsibility
in the grand scheme of things.

Some things are allowed
and some are not.   310
It's best his name
should be forgot.

Of the children of the Saki,
names we can find,
Appanoose and Black Hawk   315
and Keokuk come to mind.

Some offspring of the Mesquakie
we know
Are Poweshiek and Taimah
and Wapello.   320

For the spirit that gained
their ancestors fame,
Let us honor their brave
American names.   324

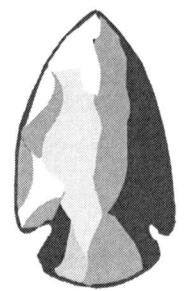

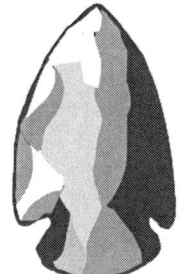

Notes

Line 1

Wapello was a tough bargainer for the Fox/Mesquakie tribe during the 1840s negotiations to sell its Iowa land to the United States government. At his request, Wapello was buried near the Indian agent in the county that bears his name. "Wap" rhymes with "top."

Line 6

The Fox were misnamed by early explorers who mistook a clan name—fox, bear, eagle—for a tribe name. This tribe of people should have been called Mesquakie.
Fox = Mesquakie

Line 14

A portage is a place where travelers take their canoe out of the water and carry it—around a waterfall, for example, or from one stream to another.

Line 26

The Fox, an Algonquin-speaking waterway/
woodland people, traveled by canoe. The
Sioux, a Siouan-speaking plains people, were
horsemen.

Line 37

The Mohawks were members of the Iroquois
Confederacy located in New York State.
Mohawk = Iroquois

Line 46

The giant 30-foot birch-bark canoes of the
fur trade were called Master or Montreal
canoes.

Line 60

Wapsipinicon is an Algonquin word for a plant that
grew along the river. "Wap" rhymes with "top."

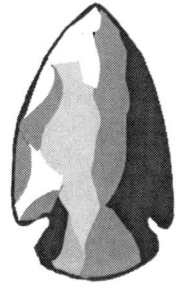

Line 67

The Sac and Fox were closely related, speaking the same dialect.

Line 101

Reports say 84 French troops and hundreds of Iroquois warriors. The records were preserved in the French state archives.

Line 104

The lack of food was emphasized in the captain's account.

Line 147

Spelled "des Moingona" on early maps, the river is named for the Moingona tribe of the Illinois Confederacy.

Line 249

The captain estimated 50 wigwams and 250 Sac and Fox warriors were across the river.

Classroom Comments

Rhyme is a learning tool of great power. In *Soaring Wings*, it dramatizes Native American and French Colonial history as well as Midwestern and Canadian geography. At the same time, the verses effortlessly vary and enrich the study of language arts. Teachers gain an opportunity to visit a multitude of diverse subjects swiftly and naturally, not unlike the nimble fingers of an accomplished pianist accenting numerous keys with both hands.

In artists of both kinds, the satisfaction of an expert performance flows from personal interest, talent, and preparation.

In a prose text, there are both chapter headings and paragraph indentations to indicate where changes of perspective occur. They add visual structure to the text and help in the design of lesson plans.

A poem, however, with its weaving rhythms and subtle rhyme patterns, may be great fun to read and a treasure when memorized, but it gives very few hints about structure. Poetry doesn't provide chapter headings, and it doesn't provide paragraph indentations as visual clues to changes of perspective.

The chart on the next page shows where all those missing chapter headings and paragraph breaks would be located in *Soaring Wings*.

For chapter headings, use the Roman numerals already printed in the poem. The eighty-one quatrains have been numbered and grouped to indicate the probable paragraph breaks.

For example, the first paragraph consists of Quatrains 1, 2, and 3; the second paragraph of Quatrains 4 and 5; and so forth. This makes a clear and convenient numbering system for organizing lesson plans and conducting class discussions.

Chapter	Paragraphs	Chapter	Paragraphs
I	1-2-3	VI	38-39-40
	4-5		41-42-43
	6-7		44-45-46
	8-9		47-48-49
II	10-11	VII	50-51-52
	12-13-14		53-54-55
	15-16-17		56-57-58
III	18-19		59-60
	20-21	VIII	61-62-63
	22-23-24		64-65-66
IV	25-26-27		67-68-69
	28-29		70-71-72
	30-31-32	IX	73-74-75
V	33-34		76-77-78
	35-36-37		79-80-81

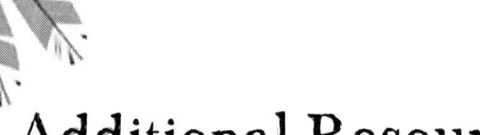

Additional Resources

The Fox Wars by R. David Edmunds and Joseph L. Peyser is an excellent resource book for teachers preparing to discuss the conflict between the French and the Sac and Fox.

Since a classroom merits art of the highest quality, consider playing sections of Anton Dvorak's famous symphony *From the New World*. Research will reveal a connection between the great composer, Native American themes, and the landscape north of the "wandering Wapsipinicon."

If you're looking for examples of the giant, thirty-foot Montreal canoes, consider paintings by Frances Hopkins. The website of the Minnesota Historical Society could be a resource.

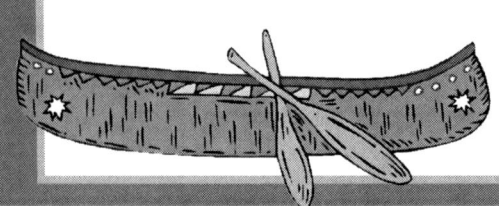

To illustrate the war victims that haunted the dreams of "the scout with second sight," consider the watercolor *Blackfeet Girl* by Karl Bodmer. She's in color in *Karl Bodmer's Studio Art* by Raymond Wood, Joseph C. Porter, and David C. Hunt. It looks like she's wearing a backpack, just as students do today.

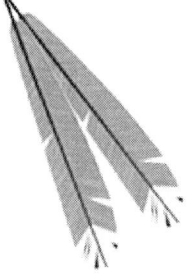

New France

West

Lake Superior

WISCONSIN

Wisconsin River

Mackinac

CHIPPEWA

SAC/FOX

Green Bay

Lake Michigan

Fox River

SIOUX

Wapsipinicon River

Des Moines River

Ioway River

Red Cedar River

Rock River

IOWA

Skunk River

Illinois River

ILLINOIS

MISSOURI

Mississippi River

New France

East

CANADA

Montreal

IROQUOIS/MOHAWK

Georgian Bay

Lake Huron

Lake Michigan

HURON

Lake Ontario

Lake Erie

...ior

UNITED STATES

CPSIA information can be obtained at www.ICGtesting.com
Printed in the USA
LVOW040711020412

275654LV00003B/1/P